THE KEY TO
CREWEL EMBROIDERY

THE KEY TO
CREWEL EMBROIDERY

The Gracious Embroidery for

Interior Decorating and Personal Items

By DOROTHY SARA

MAX PADELL, INC.
830 Broadway, New York, N.Y. 10003

ACKNOWLEDGMENTS

Appreciation is expressed to the following people for material used in this book:

The American Thread Company for basic embroidery stitches.
Hiawatha Crewel Kits for embroidery designs.
Celia Murray for original illustrations.

CONTENTS

CHAPTER   Page

INTRODUCTION   ix

1   MATERIALS FOR CREWEL WORK   1

Fabrics to use — yarns for embroidering —
needles and sizes — round frames for holding
work — rectangular frames — small piece in
large frame

2   BASIC EMBROIDERY STITCHES   9

25 basic stitches — space filling stitches — decorative border stitches — how to make a tassel

3   BEGIN WITH A SAMPLER   37

Learn by stitching a sampler — contemporary
samplers — practicing stitches — suggested
ways to combine basic stitches

4   PRESSING, BLOCKING, STRETCHING   41

To launder or clean — how to press embroidery
— blocking and stretching methods

5   TRADITIONAL CREWEL DESIGNS   44

Wall hanging — blue bird pillow — lady's handbag — wallet for handbag — eyeglass case — pillow cover design for the beginner — cat picture to be mounted or framed

6   EARLY AMERICAN DESIGNS   52

American Eagle picture — New England scenic picture to be used for home decoration

7   CONTEMPORARY AMERICAN DESIGNS   55

A chair seat — stuffed cat pillow which may be used as a toy — tote bag for the ladies

8   MAKING AND APPLYING DESIGNS   60

How to create your own designs — sources for designs — buying transfer patterns — how to reduce and enlarge size of designs by photostats — change size by use of paper ruled in squares — how to apply the design to material by basting, or prick-and-color, or carbon paper method

9   THINGS YOU CAN MAKE   72

Improvising your own designs — embroidery on dress — on jacket or sweater — on bedspread, table cloth, bell pull — embroidery on drapery and valance — how to frame an embroidered picture

INTRODUCTION

Crewel work has a long and interesting history; there are fine examples shown in art museums and historical societies in this and other countries. Our American heritage of crewel work comes from the English who brought this art with them when they first sailed here as colonists. In the sixteenth century in England crewel work was used to embellish bed coverings, curtains around beds, valances, wall hangings, and wherever in the home it was desired to add beauty. Then they used the embroidery on their petticoats and other wearing apparel.

The English traders who went to the Orient in the early days of exploration brought back with them beautiful pieces done on silk and embroidered with gold threads. The Oriental designs were usually based on their "tree of life" concept, which they embellished with birds and floral patterns. The needleworkers in England added other designs, in scroll patterns and borders. And by the seventeenth century the name of "Jacobean" was applied to crewel embroidery. Linen and similar materials were then used, and wool became the yarn most used in crewel work.

In America new designs and various materials and yarns came into use, to fit in with the colonial times, which gives us a fine heritage of Early American crewel work. And we are still originating new designs and materials for crewel work, so that we have a Contemporary American crewel which is an interesting interpretation of the ideas of today.

Crewel embroidery is a fascinating pastime for the young girl or the mature woman (or the man in the house who wants to express his art and skill). It is a relaxing and skillful way to add beauty in home decorations and add interest to fashion accessories. Crewel work is easy to learn, and it is especially helpful to the beginner as well as the experienced needleworker to know that there are kits now available which come in Old English, Early American and Contemporary American designs, to please the taste of the individual.

Dorothy Sara

Chapter One

MATERIALS FOR CREWEL WORK

You will need four basic things to produce crewel embroidery; they are: the fabric, yarn, needle, and frame for holding your work. Your choice of these will depend, of course, on the finished work you wish to produce and the design that you will embroider.

Fabrics to Use

Generally crewel work is done on Belgian linen. However, you can be flexible about the fabric you use, because you will want something of heavier texture for a chair seat and something much lighter for a bridge cloth or an embroidered jacket you will wear. Whichever fabric you choose, be sure it is of the finest quality as you will want it to be a "joy forever" thing, and it would be wasteful to devote your energy and time in embroidering on a fabric which would not be long-lasting.

You may embroider on almost any fabric you like, such as linen, cotton, wool, silk, and many of the synthetic fabrics. For great luxury, you might also work on velvet and heavy satin; although that would be for something very special, considering the fact it might be difficult to keep such luxury fabrics in good condition.

A far swing away from such fabrics is the fact that in some of the Contemporary American designs (many of which are available in kits) burlap is used as the fabric. This is usually for amusing animal and bird designs which are used for framing and hanging on the wall, and for casual colorful tote bags which women carry.

Thus, there is no hard-and-fast rule anymore about the fabric you work on; you select the one which best suits your purpose.

Yarns for Embroideries

The yarn or thread you use depends on the fabric and the design. If you buy the object of your work in a kit, the suitable yarn will be enclosed to fit the fabric. But if you do your own designing, you will find that on Belgian linen or similar fabric the 2-ply wool yarn, such as made by Hiawatha, is especially good for crewel work; it is of firm texture and does not stretch while you work. The wool yarn usually comes in small hanks so you do not need to buy large amounts.

You may do some work where you will use cotton thread, and for such purpose Star 6-strand embroidery cotton or Star pearl cotton is suitable. Some special designs may call for silk thread, to be used in 3 or 4 strands, and some contemporary designs call for yarn blended of wool and synthetic.

Needles

You may buy crewel or embroidery needles in packets of assorted sizes. They come in sizes from 3 to 8, and you choose the needle which suits the thickness of the yarn or thread which you use. Usually a #3 and #4 needle is good for crewel work, and a finer one (#5 needle) may be used for cotton or silk thread.

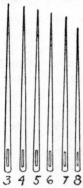

3 4 5 6 7 8

A crewel needle is not too long, but it has a long eye so it may be threaded easily. A good hint to bear in mind is that it is best to have the needle a little thicker than the thread itself, so that the needle (when inserted into the fabric) opens up a large enough hole which enables the yarn to go through smoothly.

Also include a #21 tapestry needle, for special use in surface stitches (not those which go through the fabric, such as the Whipped Running Stitch and the Spider Web Stitch where weaving needs to be done). The blunt end of the tapestry needle is helpful in such cases.

Frames for Holding Work

To aid you in attaining a smoothly finished look to your stitches, rather than to do your embroidery in a free-hand manner it is much better to work with a frame. These come in various sizes and styles, in round and rectangular shapes, and the experienced embroiderer may have a few of these frames on hand to use for different pieces on which the crewel work is done.

1. The round frame held in the hand is the simplest frame made.

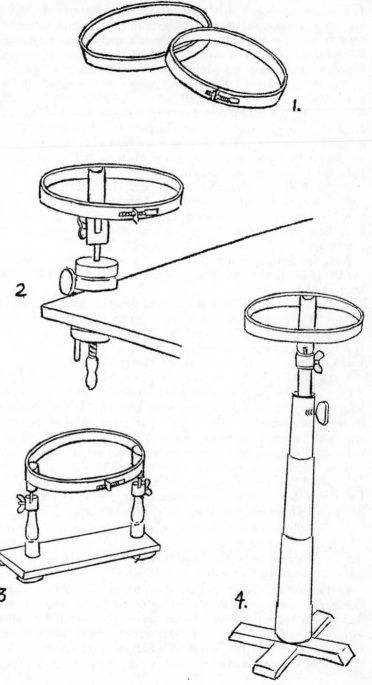

1.

2

3

4.

It consists of two hoops, the smaller size fitting into the larger size ring. They come in wood, metal or plastic, and measure from 4 to 10 inches in diameter so you have a wide range when working on different size fabric.

Some frames have no adjustable screws or clamps on them; you just push the bottom (the smaller) hoop into the upper (the larger) hoop. This may work out well with a rugged piece of fabric, but when working with more delicate material it may not do too well. In such case, it is best to get the ring frame which has a screw adjustment on the upper ring, to allow you to loosen the hoop and fit your fabric into it properly, and then to tighten the screw to hold the fabric smooth and straight.

If the fabric is delicate in weave and texture, or is of very light color and might be marked, use a piece of tissue paper which you lay over the bottom hoop, and over the paper put the fabric, and then adjust both the paper and material together into the top hoop.

Also, for delicate material, you might wind a soft binding around the lower hoop, then put the material over that, and adjust the top hoop over it.

If you are working on a very small piece of material, which you cannot fit into the frame, a good suggestion is to baste the piece of material to be embroidered on a larger piece of linen or other sturdy cotton fabric. Then insert that into the two hoops, and you can do your embroidering on the small piece.

2. Here is a facile way of using the hoops, by screwing the frame with a clamp to the edge of a table to which you can draw your chair while doing your crewel work. Or it may be clamped to the arm of a chair if you find that more convenient. And this may also be clamped to the edge of a small table which you can move about, to wherever you prefer to sit while embroidering.

This also has a screw adjustment which enables it to be raised or lowered to a desired height. An advantage here is that you have free use of both hands, rather than needing to hold the frame with one hand while you can work only with the other hand.

3. The frame held on the lap may be convenient for your use. The frame has screws at both sides, so you may tilt the hoops to any angle which is best for you to use. You may also set this on a table and work in that manner.

4. The advantage of this standing frame is that you may carry the frame to any place in the house or outdoors, where you enjoy doing your crewel work. This has screw adjustment for raising or lowering the height of the hoops, also a screw which allows for tilting the angle of the hoops to whatever position is comfortable for you to do your work.

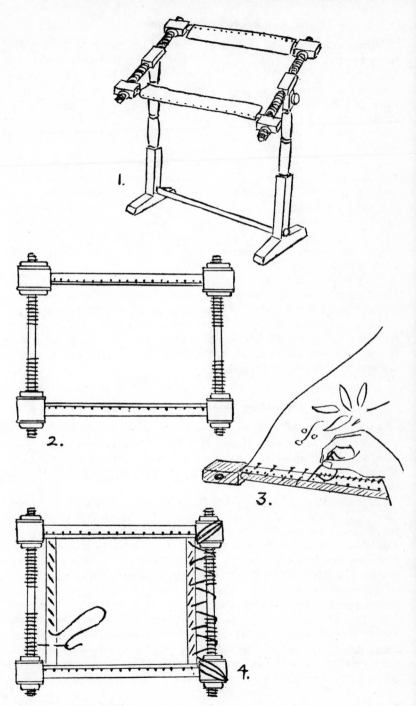

1.

2.

3.

4.

Rectangular Frames

When you work on something that is too large to be handled with a small hoop ring, you may use a square frame which can accomodate larger pieces. If you are working on a large surface, such as a bedspread or wall hanging, and you want to keep it open so you may see and enjoy the design as it is done in its entirety, you might find the square frame too small. In such case, you might use your do-it-yourself ingenuity and construct your own frame to accomodate the large piece.

1. The rectangular frame shown here is the usual one, which has two adjustable screw-sides, and the other two sides with rollers (which are used at the top and bottom of the frame). On top of the rollers a webbing is nailed down, to which you sew down the fabric which you are embroidering. Illustrated here is the frame with a floor stand, with screw adjustment to enable you to tilt the frame to the angle you desire. This is the most convenient way with which to work your embroidery.

2. You may have a frame held in your hand (without a floor stand), and you may prop it against a large chair or you may devise some other manner of holding it on a table or in your lap.

An advantage in using a square frame is that some fabrics may be damaged by marks left on their surface by the hoops of a ring frame, yet you could work with them in the rectangular frame without such harm to the fabric.

Mounting Embroidery on Frame

As the material (on which you are embroidering) is to be stretched on this square frame, if it has any selvedges it is a good idea to use the point of your small scissors to make snips through the selvedge, about 1 inch apart, so the material will fit flatly and not be restrained.

First unscrew the two rollers (which are covered with webbing) from the sides, so they are free from the frame. Make a pencil mark in the center of each roller. Now turn under the top edge of the fabric, about a quarter of an inch, and crease the fabric between your fingers. Put a pin in the center of the width of the material, where you have creased over the fold, and match this pin to the pencil mark on the roller, then pin the material to the webbing of the roller at that center spot.

3. Sew the folded edge of the material to the webbing of the roller. Use a heavy-duty cotton or linen thread and start to sew from the center where the fabric is pinned to the webbing. Use very small, short stitches (whip stitch) and make a strong tacking when you come to the end of the row. Then start the other side,

again at the pinned-down center, and sew the rest of the folded-over fabric to the webbed roller.

Now do the same with the other roller. Fold under the other edge of the material and put a pin in the center. Make sure to match the pin exactly to the pencil mark on the roller, so that it is even with the sewed-on material on the opposite roller. Then start at the center and sew down each side of the folded material (as you did on the other roller).

You are now ready to assemble the frame. Put the two screw-sides into the slots on both rollers, then adjust the nuts until the material is held as tightly as possible with the frame. Make sure that the top of the design is placed on the top roller, or else you'll have to work your design upside down. To be positive that the material is equally placed in the frame, measure each screw-side so that they are both the same length. When you are sure that the fabric is properly in place, make the frame secure by putting back the outer screws.

4. It is now necessary to attach the two sides of the material to the frame. Start by sewing a very heavy tape or a strip of webbing under each side of the material. As this will have to take a lot of strain, be sure the tape is sewed down (with a diagonal stitch or a cross stitch) with extra-heavy cotton or linen thread. Or, you might roll the edge of the material over a heavy cord, and sew that down, and the cord will act as a strengthener.

Now, use a curved upholsterer's needle and a fine but strong string to attach the material to the sides of the frame. Start lacing this string at the top of the side of the frame, and work down to the bottom, and secure it very tightly around the frame. If you use a tape or webbing, sew the lacing through that. Or, if you used the rolled-under cord, sew the lacing within the corded edge. When doing this lacing process, make sure to keep the stitches evenly to insure the material is flat and taut. If, during the process of your working on it, some part of the lacing becomes loosened, you tighten it either by pulling the lacing and tacking it where necessary, or by turning the screw on the frame.

Small Piece in Large Frame

You may want to embroider a piece that is very small and cannot be fitted into the rectangular frame. In such case mount into the square frame a piece of material that is very sturdy (such as denim or linen), using the sewing-on and lacing-to method outlined in the foregoing instructions. Then, when this material is taut and smooth within the frame, lay down in the center your small piece to be worked on. With a running stitch sew this down onto the material encased in the frame, tacking it securely so it will remain flat and smooth while you embroider it. When the design is finished, you just have to rip the small piece off. It might be a good idea to let the strong piece of fabric remain within the frame, in case you have any other small piece you want to embroider in the near future.

Chapter Two

BASIC EMBROIDERY STITCHES

We show here the embroidery stitches which are the A-B-C of crewel work. You may want to experiment in trying out combinations of the stitches. Also you may sometimes find a magazine article on crewel embroidery which refers to a stitch which you do not find here, and in the kits of crewel work you buy you may find some interesting stitches and their usage will be explained to you in the instruction sheet in the kit.

But when you use these stitches in your work, you will have a very good basis of procedure to produce fine results. Some stitches are more adaptable than others to certain materials and yarns, but as you become more experienced in crewel work you will be able to determine which are best for your use.

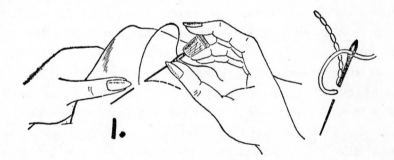

1. **Back Stitch.** This stitch is worked from right to left. Bring the needle out on the right side of the material. Then insert the needle ⅛ inch to the right, and bring it out again ⅛ inch to the left (in front of the first stitch). Now insert the needle through the same hole where the thread was first brought out, and bring needle up again ⅛ inch to the left. Continue in the same manner.

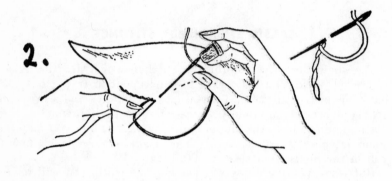

2. Outline Stitch. Work this stitch from left to right. Bring the needle out on the right side of material. Then insert the needle a little further along to the right. Hold the thread with the left thumb, bring needle out again half way between. Hold the thread with left thumb, and insert the needle a little further along the line to be covered. Bring the needle up in the same hole at the end of the last stitch. Always hold the thread with your left thumb to the left side. The effect is slightly different if the thread is held to the right side. It is important to hold the thread to the same side from start to finish.

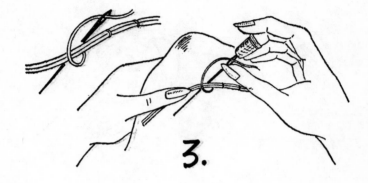

3. **Couching Stitch.** Place one or two threads along the couching line. Sew these threads in place with small stitches, either in the same or a contrasting color. Always have the stitches an equal distance apart.

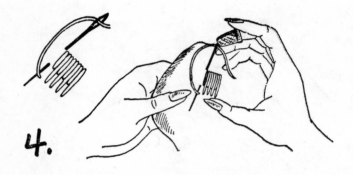

4.

4. **Long and Short Stitch.** This is sometimes called the **Kensington Stitch.** This is made by working one long and one short straight stitch, close to one another. This is used to fill in solid areas, and to produce a shading of colors. Sometimes different tones of one color, or some blending colors, are used in alternating rows of this stitch. It is often possible to produce interesting color effects by doing the first row the darkest shade, and then each succeeding row (under each other) a lighter shade.

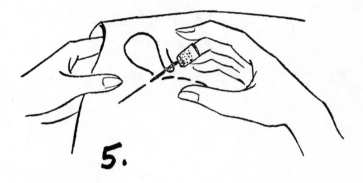

5.

5. **Running Stitch.** A short, even stitch which is made by passing the needle over and under the material, in even distance. Or you may vary this by making the stitch (on the bottom of the fabric) shorter than the stitch on right side of the fabric; but in any case they must be kept to even length.

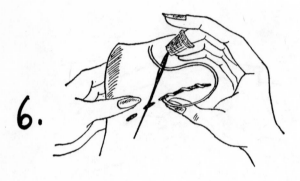

6.

6. **Whipped Running Stitch.** This is an elaboration of the running stitch. The needle does not go through the material, but it is inserted under and over the running stitches. This could be with a thread of the same color, or with a contrasting color. As this needle does not go through the material, it might be easier for you to do this whipping by using a blunt-end tapestry needle.

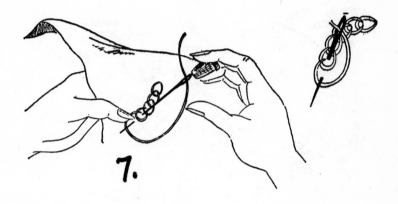

7. **Chain Stitch.** Bring the thread to the right side of the material. Hold the thread down with left thumb, and insert the needle (held in your right hand) into the same hole, then bring the needle up about ¼ inch below. Repeat as before.

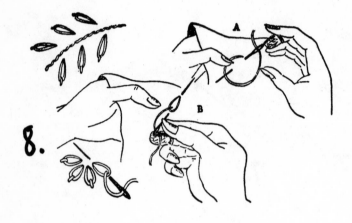

8. **Lazy Daisy Stitch.** This is worked in the same way as the chain stitch "A" and is kept in position by a small stitch in the center at the round end of loop "B".

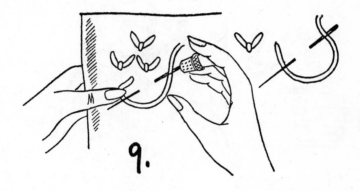

9. **Fly Stitch.** Bring the thread to the right side. Hold the thread under left thumb. Insert the needle a small distance to the right. Then bring the needle up over the thread and about ¼ inch below the previous stitches. Fasten the stitch with a small straight stitch. Bring the thread out again at the same level as the first stitch made, and a small distance to the right. Continue as before.

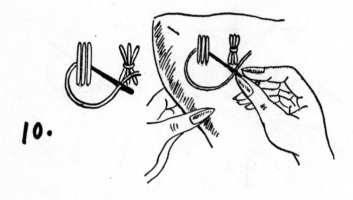

10.

10. **Bundle Stitch.** This is also called **Faggot Stitch.** The stitch is made up of three or four straight stitches, brought together in the center with a tight overcasting stitch. You may use the same thread to tie the bundles, or a contrasting color to produce an attractive effect.

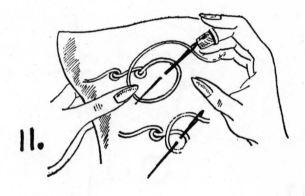

11. Scroll Stitch. Work this stitch from left to right. Bring the thread to the right side of the material. Form a loop from right to left, holding the loop down with left thumb. Pick up a small amount of the material in the center of the loop. Bring the needle up and release the loop slowly. This stitch is most effective when you use a heavy yarn.

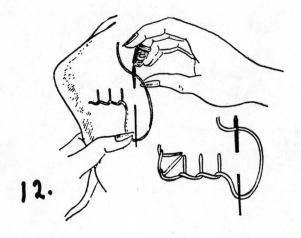

12. **Blanket Stitch.** Bring the thread to the right side on the lower edge. Then insert the needle about ¼ inch above, and to the right. Now bring the needle out above the loop which is held by the thumb. Continue in the same manner.

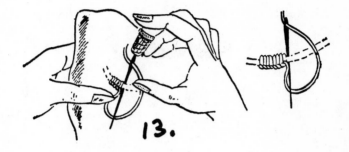

13.

13. **Buttonhole Stitch.** Make this stitch in the same way you do the blanket stitch, with the exception that the stitches must be worked close to each other.

14.

14. **Scallops.** Work this stitch in a close buttonhole stitch (basically the blanket stitch), starting narrow and getting wider in the center of the scallop.

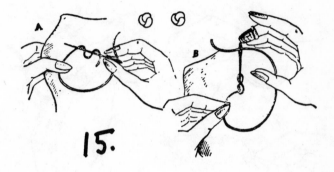

15. **French Knot.** Bring the thread to the right side. Hold thread with left hand (A), then twist the thread around the needle twice (or 3 or 4 times, depending on the size knot desired). Insert the needle (B) to wrong side, holding the knot in place with the left thumb.

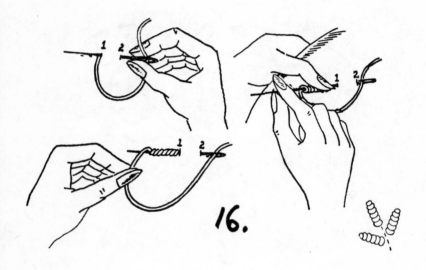

16. **Bullion Stitch.** This is sometimes called the **Bullion Knot.**
Bring out the thread at "1" as shown in illustration. Stitch back to
"2". Then come out at "1" again, leaving the needle in the material.
Twist the thread around the needle, making enough twists to cover
the length of the stitch. Hold the twist in place with your left
thumb, and ease the needle through gently. Stitch down through
"2" and the stitch is then completed.

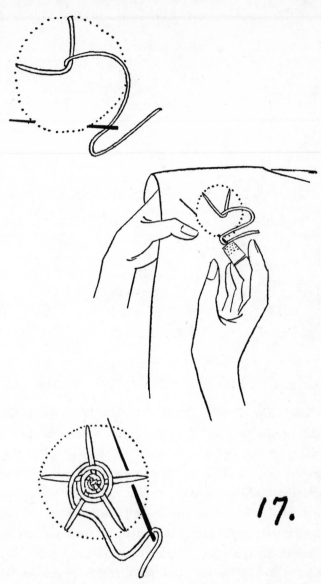

17.

17. **Spider Web Stitch.** Begin this with a fly stitch to the center of the circle. Then work two straight stitches, making one on each side of the fly stitch "tail" into the center of the circle. You now have five equal divisions of the circle, and the web is made up of the spokes. To form the web, use a tapestry needle with a blunt end (as the needle does not go through the material), and weave under and over the spokes until you have made a whole spider web.

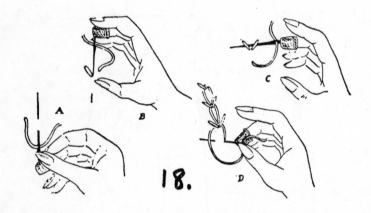

18. **Wheat Ear Stitch.** Bring the thread to the right side. Insert the needle diagonally to the right, below the line. Bring the needle up again diagonally to the right (A) and at the same height as the first stitch. Insert needle again diagonally to the left "B" forming a V. Now bring the needle out below V in the length of stitch desired. Slip the needle through 2 stitches "C" forming the V, without stitching through the material. Insert the needle back where thread emerged last. Bring the needle out slightly higher "D" and diagonally to the left. Insert the needle in base of stitch, and continue as before.

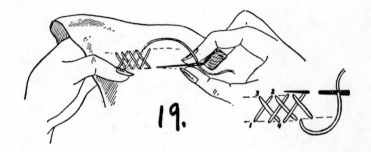

19. **Herringbone Stitch.** This stitch is worked along a double line, from left to right. Bring out the needle at (1), then insert needle at (2), and bring the needle out at (3), and insert it at (4). Continue in the same way.

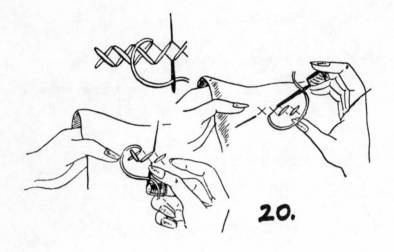

20. **Cross Stitch.** Bring out the thread at the bottom of the
cross. Stitch up diagonally from left to right. Bring out the needle
at the bottom of the next cross. Work all the stitches in the same
direction first. Then work all the top stitches in he opposite direction. When finished, the crosses should join at the top and bottom.

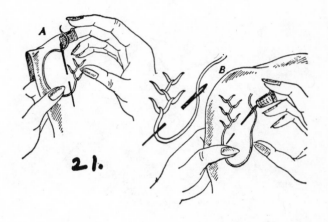

21. **Feather Stitch.** Bring thread to the right side. Hold thread with left thumb, and insert the needle above and to the left. Bring the needle out over the working thread "A". Hold the thread down with left thumb, and insert the needle above and to the right "B". Now bring the needle out over the working thread. Continue in this way, once to the left and once to the right of the center.

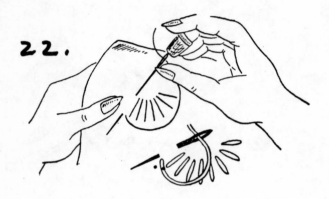

22. Straight Stitch. This stitch is worked by one single stitch in a straight line taken over a small portion of the material. The stitches may sometimes be of varying size, and may be done in a regular or irregular manner.

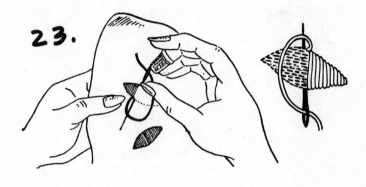

23. Satin Stitch. This stitch is used to fill a design. First pad the design with small running stitches before starting the satin stitch. Bring the needle out at lower edge. Work a straight stitch by inserting the needle at the upper edge, then bringing the needle out again at the lower edge close beside the first stitch. This stitch can be worked either straight or slanting, but it must always be worked close together.

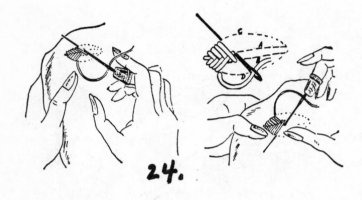

24.

24. **Fish Bone Stitch.** This is sometimes called the **Dorondo Stitch.** Draw two lines ⅛ inch apart, down the center of the form to be filled. Bring out the thread at the point of the form. Make a short straight stitch down the center, bringing out the thread at the top edge of "D". Take a diagonal stitch to "A". Bring out the thread at the top edge of "C" and take a diagonal stitch to "B". Continue as before, making sure the stitches are close and next to one another.

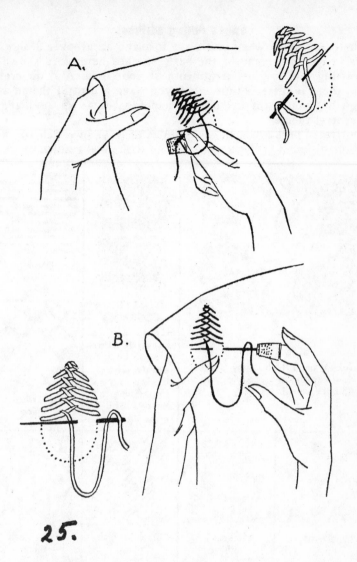

A.

B.

25.

25. Cretan Stitch. You may work this stitch in a very close, slanting form; or if it could be done with spaces between the stitches. To make the stitch, bring the needle through at top center, then take a small stitch at the right side. Now take a stitch at the left side, with the needle pointing inward and the thread under the point of the needle (A). In the same way, take a stitch on the right side (B). Continue doing this from side to side, until the form is entirely filled.

Space Filling Stitches

There are times when you want to make an all-over design, or want to combine some of the basic stitches heretofore shown in interesting and original treatments of your own. And, in crewel work, there is often a time when you have a central theme as a design but you want to "fill in" some spaces as an auxiliary to the central theme.

Illustrated here are some suggestions of ways in which you may combine different stitches and come up with good results.

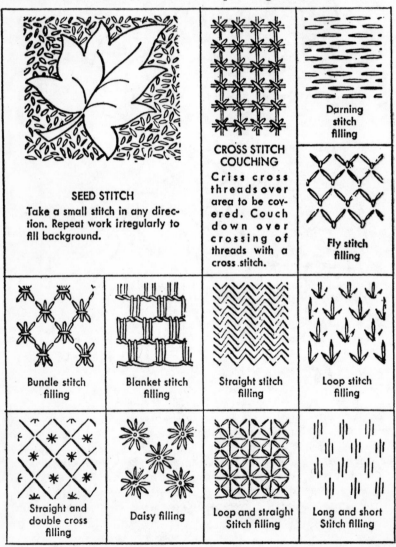

SEED STITCH
Take a small stitch in any direction. Repeat work irregularly to fill background.

CROSS STITCH COUCHING
Criss cross threads over area to be covered. Couch down over crossing of threads with a cross stitch.

Darning stitch filling

Fly stitch filling

Bundle stitch filling

Blanket stitch filling

Straight stitch filling

Loop stitch filling

Straight and double cross filling

Daisy filling

Loop and straight Stitch filling

Long and short Stitch filling

Decorative Borders

In some of your crewel work you may want to give a finished look by applying borders, such as on draperies, tablecloths, valances, bedspreads, and other decorating items; also you may want to use borders on wearing apparel.

The simple borders, shown in the accompanying illustration, are easy to achieve. You may combine two different basic stitches, and use the same or contrasting color of yarns for special effects if you wish to express individuality in your work.

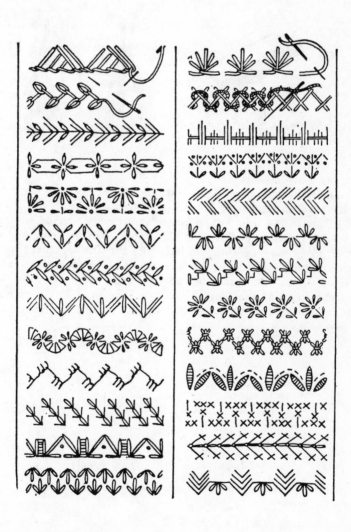

How to Make a Tassel

While this is not a stitch, the tassel is included here because it is often used for trimming. For instance, a cushion may have a tassel at each corner, or you may have a row of tassels at the end of a stole, or a tassel at the end of an embroidered bell pull.

Usually the dominant color of the crewel work is used in the tassel, and of course the same yarn (or perhaps a heavier yarn) is used to make it.

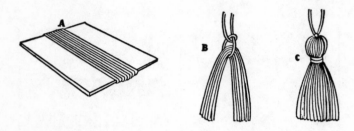

To make the tassel, wind yarn around a piece of cardboard "A", which board is cut to the length of the tassel you desire. If you want to produce a heavy tassel, wind more yarn around the cardboard; if a light tassel then wind less yarn. Cut one end, slide off the cardboard very carefully to keep the threads together, and tie a knot around the middle of the threads "B". Then wind yarn about five times around the tassel "C" about ⅜ inch below the knot. This forms the head of the tassel. To tack this so it holds securely, stitch the end of the thread several times through the head.

Chapter Three

BEGIN WITH A SAMPLER

Through the entire history of embroidery, we find that making of samplers (or "examplars") was considered a popular pastime for the needleworker. Often the sampler showed the letters of the alphabet, as a practice piece of embroidery. Some samplers were actually charts showing the genealogical "family tree" worked in embroidery and the names of the ancestors sewed into the leaves of the tree.

Children made samplers, often with a motto from the Holy Bible or some charming sentiment like "God bless our home" and the date and initials of the embroiderer worked into the stitches.

By now some of these lovely samplers have become collector's items, they are found in museums and they are handed down as heirlooms in families.

Contemporary Samplers

You may want to do some practice working of stitches before you start out to do an important piece of household decoration, or a personal accessory for yourself. The easiest way is to try one with Belgian linen and fine 2-ply crewel wool. And you can make another sampler, using a more delicate material and perhaps an embroidery cotton or other kind of yarn.

In making such samplers you will get the "feel" of handling the needle, and you may originate some simple patterns to work out. Suggested in these illustrations are two samplers, made up of combinations of basic embroidery outline stitches and space-filling stitches, which are described in the previous chapter.

You may use various colors of yarn, and then use these samplers as original wall decorations. Some samplers are made in picture form, and may be mounted or framed.

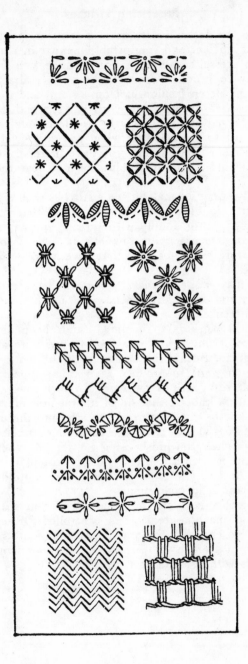

Practicing Stitches

Aside from the decorative value of a sampler, it enables you to find the most efficient and comfortable manner in which you may perform your crewel embroidery. For instance, you will learn that the best way to produce good results is to stab the needle in straight up and down fashion, not on a slant, and not try to sew the way one does dressmaking with basting and other stitches which are achieved by "running" the needle through the material.

Another thing to know is that when you do crewel work which is held in an embroidery frame, you have better control over the needle if you hold it near the point and not near the eye of the needle.

You will also practice making some stitches with a single thread as well as with double thread. You may find that you like some stitches done singly or doubly with thread; you can find this out only when you are practicing on your sampler or on any scrap of material before you embark on the crewel work project you may have in mind.

Also, you may want to make some stitches smaller than are usually done, and some stitches larger. This too is a matter of taste and preference.

If the crewel work is to be lined (and the underside of the embroidery not visible) you may start to sew with a knot at the end of the thread. But, if the underside of the work will be seen (not lined) you want to produce as neat an appearance as you achieve on the right side of the work. In such cases, do not start the thread with a knot at the end of it. But first make a few tiny stitches with the beginning thread, directly into the material, in a safe place where you will cover the beginning stitches by the embroidery. And when you finish using the thread, whether you did or did not start it with a knotted end, you complete the stitching by running a few tiny stitches back into the embroidery, and the end of the thread is inconspicuous.

It is wise, too, to regulate the "tension" of your stitches (in the way a sewing machine tension is controlled). Keep the same tightness or looseness of the stitching throughout the work you are doing. Do not make some stitches tighter or looser than the others, as this will result in an uneven finish.

Chapter Four

PRESSING, BLOCKING, STRETCHING

To launder or not to launder, to use water or not to use water, is a matter of much puzzlement to the embroiderer. Some yarns and some materials may not lend themselves to water; they may not be color-fast or their textures may not stand up well through wetting (and soaps and detergents). Therefore, if you are not sure of the ability of your crewel work to withstand laundering, you are much wiser in sending it to a professional cleaner when it is necessary to refresh the embroidery if it has become soiled.

Some people use carbon tetrachloride or similar cleaning fluids to go over the soiled spots; but this too we hesitate to recommend, and it is up to you to decide (after practicing on a small "sampler" piece) whether to take the chance of a do-it-yourself cleaning job or relying on the services of a professional cleaning establishment.

Pressing Embroidery

While blocking is preferable (directions are given later in this chapter) there are some pieces of crewel work which may fare better with pressing. This holds true in cases where you have hemmed or fringed edges on the material. In blocking, the edges would have to take the risk of nail holes, so pressing has to be done with such embroidered articles.

Also pressing needs to be done on an embroidered design on a dress, jacket, sweater, or any other finished article which cannot be stretched and blocked by a nailing-down process. When you finish pressing the embroidery on such an article, do not fold it. Instead, hang it upon a clothes hanger, or over a rod, so as not to crush the stitches in any way or flatten them down.

Pressing should be done lightly, as too much pressure of the iron tends to flatten down the stitches and spoils the beauty of your work. If you did your crewel work with the use of a frame, the finished article may need no pressing (or very little pressing). But if you held the embroidery work in your hand, without a frame, the chances are that the finished article is in need of pressing.

On your ironing board or table top, place an extra soft, thick padding (a clean blanket is very good). On this padded surface lay the embroidered article, face down. Then, over the article place a damp, clean cloth. Very gently pass the iron over the cloth.

If you are not to use the embroidered article right away, do not fold it; instead, roll it around a cardboard tube smoothly but not too tightly so the stitches will not be crushed. Wrap tissue paper around the roll to keep it clean until the time when you will use the article.

If the embroidery you pressed is to be framed as a picture, mount it on a cardboard at once (as instructed in Chapter Nine) to prevent it becoming creased again. If you are not going to frame it at once, wrap the mounted article in tissue paper until you are ready to hang it on your wall.

Blocking, Stretching

Use a board, or the top of an old table if you don't mind hammering tacks into it, for the purpose of blocking and stretching your finished piece of crewel work.

Cover the surface (the board, or old table) with a clean sheet or other cloth. On top of this place the embroidered article. Hammer a small tack at each of the four corners, then stretching the article tautly add tacks in the center of each side, then keep on adding tacks until you have the embroidered article stretched and smoothly even.

With a clean sponge soaked in cold water, dampen the entire surface of the tacked-down article, making it evenly wet. Permit the article to become thoroughly dry (and no creases in the material) before you pull out the tacks and remove it from the table. If you find that you want it to be more smooth than the blocking has produced, you may renew the cold-water sponging and let the article dry until you get the smoothly-finished result you desire.

If you are not to use the article at once, to hang it or mount it in some manner, then roll it around a cardboard tube, and wrap tissue paper around it. Do not roll too tightly, in order to avoid crushing or flattening the crewel stitches.

Or, if you are to use the article for a framed picture, mount it at once on the cardboard, as explained in this chapter in the pressing instructions.

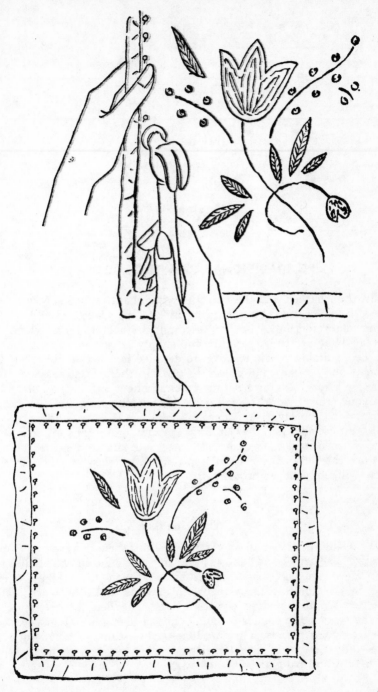

43

Chapter FIVE

TRADITIONAL CREWEL DESIGNS

In this chapter, and the two following chapters, are shown some designs which may be purchased in kits, all ready for you to do your embroidering. The kits contain the material on which is already stamped the design, the full supply of yarn in various colors needed, suitable needle to use, and detailed instruction sheet telling you which stitches and colors to use. So there is no way of you making any errors or needing to experiment before you start to do your crewel work. Usually the material is linen, and the yarns pure wool; however, in some special cases (perhaps in some of the stuffed pillows) the kit may contain other kind of material and yarn. But in each case the fabric and yarn and needle in the kit are carefully chosen to be appropriate for the design on which you will do your embroidering.

Wall Hanging

This design is a stylized version of the Oriental "Tree of Life" design. The trunk and limbs of the tree are done in shades of tan and brown, the leaves in various shades of green (the stitches blending in the colors), the bunches of grapes and the acorns and thistles are in blending shades of red, the deer at the bottom of the tree also in shades of tan. Tones of blue and orange are also used as color blends. This produces a beautiful wall hanging, in the traditional style. The kit also includes instructions as to how to mount and hang the finished work on your wall.

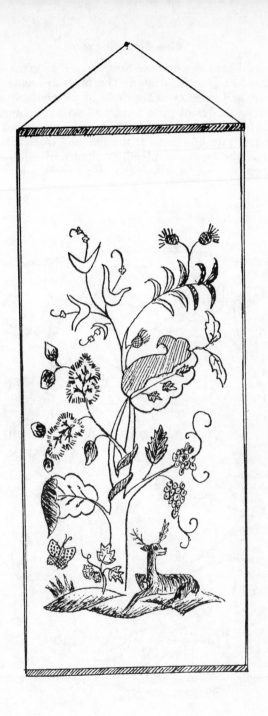

Blue Bird Pillow

In traditional crewel work the bird is used to great extent, as it does lend itself to graceful design. The birds are done in blending tones of blue, and their eyes are done in yellow, and some of the birds also have shades of pink combined with the blue. Each bird is done in different stitching and color combinations, which adds to the interest and attractiveness of the finished work. The stems are in brown, and the leaves in blending shades of light greens. The cord which goes around the finished pillow is in a lovely shade of blue.

Handbag

Very handsome accessories may be worked in the traditional style, and this purse is an example of how you may do this. The flowers are in blending colors of yellow, orange, pinks, reds. Some flowers are in light blue shades. The stems are in brown, and the leaves in blended colors of greens. In the kit is also included the instruction on making and mounting the bag, after you have finished the embroidery.

Wallet for your Handbag

If you want to carry out the theme in the dollar-bill wallet, as in the handbag, this is also available in a kit all ready for you to embroider. The color and design follow the same as the handbag itself. Also included are instructions on how to sew the wallet and its lining when you have finished doing the crewel work.

Eyeglass Case

To complete your pretty accessorizing, you might want to include the eyeglass case to match the handbag and its wallet. The

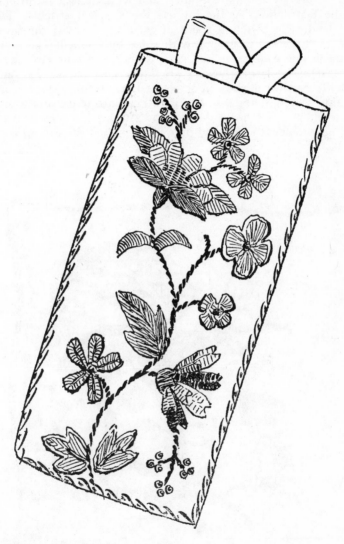

design and color are the same as the other two pieces in this set. The kit also includes instruction sheet on how to finish and sew the eyeglass case when the embroidery is completed.

For the Beginner

A Pillow Cover Design

This is expressly for the beginner, and while it is a traditional design the instructions in the kit use the simplest stitches. The little squirrel is in blending tones of gold and brown; the large leaf and its stems are in brown, with some blue added. The other leaves are in tones of green, and some brown and blue (to match the big leaf). The larger flowers are in various red shades, and some of the smaller flowers in tones of blue. While easy to embroider this design, it turns out to be a most attractive and useful article to add to your home decoration. The kit includes instructions on how to sew the finished pillow and to add the edging cord around it.

Cat Picture

While this could fit into a contemporary decorating theme, actually it is a traditional design. The cat is done in tones of olive green, some browns, a bit of orange, and they all blend in to make a most stimulating picture. The eyes are done in blue and turquoise, the nose and mouth of a light orange-red, and the scroll stitches (a couching stitch) which "frame" the cat are also of an orange-red. When the embroidery is finished, the picture is then treated in the way described at the end of Chapter Nine which tells how to frame a picture. Or you may not want to frame it, but just to mount the picture on a plywood board, and this is told in the kit's instruction sheet.

Chapter Six

EARLY AMERICAN DESIGNS

You may use Early American motifs on any article of home decoration, or clothes or accessories, if you so desire. The same stitches and blending of colors is used, as in traditional crewel work. The only difference is that the designs use the themes which were developed in the early days of our country. In this chapter we show only a few; but there are many designs of this period which you may buy in kits or devise yourself.

American Eagle Picture

The shield, of course, is done in vertical stripes of red and white, and its top border is of blue. This follows the coloring of our flag. The head of the eagle is outlined in the same red shade, and its beak is of gold. The wings and legs and claws of the bird are in blending tones of yellow, orange, gold and olive green. The little

flowers around the eagle's head are of light blue with cream white centers; the motto is in dark olive green, and the border of the scroll (held in the bird's mouth) is of medium brown. The arrow sticks are of brown, the heads and tails of the arrows are in tones of blue. The stem in the other claw is brown, the leaves in tones of green and blue. The colors blend in very well, and the result is a majestic picture. The instruction sheet in the kit tells how to block and frame the finished picture, and it is well for you to refer also to the end of Chapter Nine which tells how to frame a picture.

New England Picture

Here is a charming design which, while it portrays a New England scene, also has a delicate Chinese feeling about it. The curved

lines of the ground, at the bottom of the picture, go from light green to darker shades of green and then into a dark blue. The trees are in tones of brown and green and a touch of blue. The fishing pond is done in blue, and the ducks of course in cream white and touches of other colors. The man and woman have red in their costumes, the chimneys are red, the house in tones of green and some brown, and the sky of course is a lovely sky-blue. When completed this is a colorful yet serene picture. The kit includes instruction for blocking and framing the picture, and your attention is also directed to the end of Chapter Nine which discusses how to frame an embroidered picture.

Chapter Seven

CONTEMPORARY AMERICAN DESIGNS

While you follow the same basic stitching and methods of procedure as in the traditional crewel work, you may adapt your designs to current ideas, and for usages which the early embroiderers never dreamed of. In this chapter we show some ways of applying crewel embroidery to contemporary designs; you may want to buy kits or originate your own patterns to express your modern ideas.

Chair Seat

Here is a simple, modern way to embroider a seat for a chair. The cherries are worked in colors blending from light coral to dark rose. The big stem is in tones of brown and gray-green. The leaves are embroidered in tones of green and yellow. The bees are gold and brown and light gray-green; the butterflies are in various colors such as brown and turquoise, and gold and red. While there is a variance of colors, the finished effect is fairly muted. The kit instruction sheet tells how to block and press before the embroidered seat is attached to the chair.

This idea may be carried out in a couch or love-seat, or you may also want to make a back to the chair (if it has both an upholstered back as well as seat).

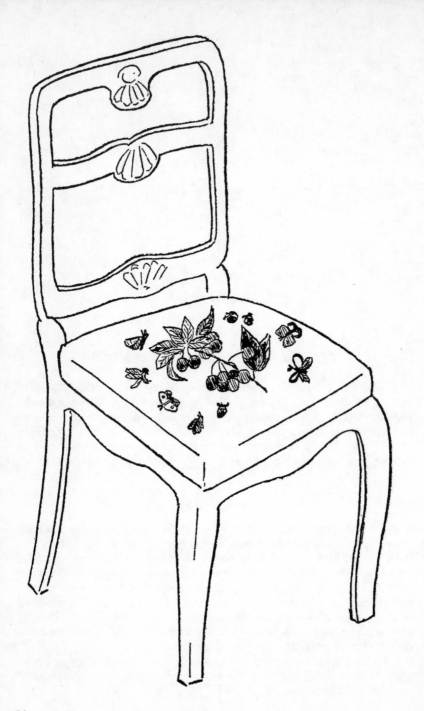

Stuffed Cat Pillow

This is an amusing pillow to be used in a contemporary room; or a child might even want this as a toy. The design is embroidered in various shades of yellow and orange and red. The ears and the three top pieces of hair on the cat's face are done in a dark red shade; the nose and mouth of orange, the whiskers are yellow. The center of the eyes is a dark red shade, and the outer ends of both eyes are in gold. The fabric which comes in the kit is of a green-beige-brown tone, so that the embroidery colors show up very well on the material. The back of the cat is embroidered the same

as the front. A cardboard base is included too, which you use when sewing the cat together (when you proceed to stuff it). The base enables the cat to sit up straight.

Tote Bag

Now that the tote bag has become part of accessorizing a costume, aside from its utility value, you may want to embroider a bag and show that you can adapt traditional crewel work to fit your today's tastes. The big wheel is done in light and dark shades of yellow and orange. This same orange is used to outline the bag as well as the handles. The smaller wheel is done in a dark pink and outlined in wine color; while the little flowers inside that wheel are done in a light pink. The leaves are done in light to dark shades of green, and the snail's round contour is in two shades of light green while its "body" is in a wine shade. Full directions on how to sew the bag, and put in a lining and affix the handles, are given in the kit's instruction sheet.

Chapter EIGHT

MAKING AND APPLYING DESIGNS

When you want to create your own designs, there is no limit to the places and the things which will be inspirations to you. Of course it depends on what you want to make, whether it be a design for a home decorating item, or a fashion accessory.

You may see a lovely bunch of flowers in a vase in the window of a florist's shop, or you may receive an attractive greeting card (for your birthday or other occasion) in the mail, which could provide you with the theme of a design. You might see a piece of drapery or dress fabric or a wallpaper, which has a design in it you might want to adapt to a pattern for embroidery.

The color of the yarn you use will also be suggested to you by these same sources of inspiration for crewel designs. Or, if you have a favorite color, let it be the basic hue around which you choose the yarn colors to blend with it. Experiment with various colors of yarns by making practice stitches on scraps of material. A lovely design may appear one way with the use of some colors, and yet give a different effect when the yarns are of other colors. You may find the color scheme you want by putting together skeins of yarn of the colors you like, and then shifting the skeins around until you find the right blend of colors and the positions in which you want to use them when embroidering the pattern on the material.

Buying Transfer Patterns

The firms who make paper sewing patterns often make embroidery transfer patterns too, and you may find a design you like in those ready-made patterns. However, they may be too small or too large for your purposes, and in the following is told how you may adapt a design to a smaller or larger size as required.

Reducing and Enlarging Designs

If you have a design (which you were able to acquire or perhaps to draw it yourself) and want to use it on an area where it would be necessary to either reduce or enlarge that design, before transferring it to the material to be embroidered, there are several ways in which you can make the pattern fit the space you have available.

Use Photostat Service

There may be a service in your locality where you can have a photostatic reproduction made of the design you have, and it can be reduced or enlarged to the size you need. For instance, if the pattern you have is only 4 by 6 inches, but you want it to be 6 by 8 inches (to make a larger design on what you want to embroider), the photostat can be made to that size. Or, if the pattern you have is 12 by 14 inches, but the area you need to work on will allow for a pattern of only 6 by 9 inches, the photostat service could reduce it for you.

If you do not find such a service listed in the telephone directory in your area, you might inquire of the nearest public library or an advertising agency or a legal office near you, as such places use photostatic services and could undoubtedly provide you with such a firm's name.

After you get the photostat in the size you need, use a tracing paper over the photostat and mark the pattern on it, for use in transferring it to the article to be embroidered.

The photostat comes in a negative (black paper with white lines over it), and then they make a positive (white paper with black lines). It is just as easy to trace from the negative, so do not order a positive unless you want to do so. Thus you will save money, as often they charge one fee for the negative, then an extra cost for making the positive print.

Changing Size by Use of Squares

1. Whether you want to reduce or enlarge the design, the procedure is the same. With a ruler, measure off and draw equal squares on the design; this could be four or more squares. Have the same proportion in the small and the large paper. Then very carefully draw into each square the lines of the pattern; either

from the larger size to the smaller for purpose of reduction, or from the smaller size to the larger to enlarge the design. This is not hard to do; all it requires is patience.

2. Another way is to use graph paper, which is available at

1.

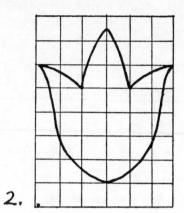

2.

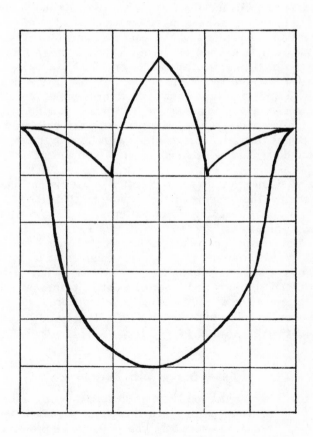

an artists' supply store, or at a stationery shop. This paper comes with printed small squares, and here also you make either a reduced or an enlarged design (drawing the lines either for smaller or larger squares, to be in proportion to the squares from which you are drawing). Then proceed as instructed in the foregoing paragraph.

Also buy a good quality tracing paper, so when you have the final pattern (whether it be a photostat or a design on cloth or paper) you will then put the tracing paper over it, and with pencil draw the design. And from this tracing paper you will then proceed to transfer the design on to the fabric.

Applying the Design

The three methods mostly used for transferring the design from the tracing paper on to the material on which you are to embroider are: by basting, by pricking and coloring, and by drawing over carbon paper. The method used will depend in large measure on the thinness or thickness of the fabric on which you work, as well as on the size and shape of the article. For instance, when transferring a design to a stole or a sweater or a dress, or to a large article such as a wall hanging or bedspread, you may find one method more preferable than another. And the only way to determine this is through experimenting with these transfer methods until you determine which one is most convenient for you to handle.

On sheer fabrics you may find it better to use the basting method, rather than the pricking or the carbon-paper method.

If you buy ready-made transfer patterns (put out commercially by pattern companies), these three methods may not need to be used, as the instructions with the pattern tell you how to lay it down on the material and to press the design right on to the material. However, if the bought transfer pattern is not of the size you want, and you have to reduce or enlarge it, then you will not be able to follow the direct pressing-on instructions, but will need to use one of the following three methods after you have made the final design on the tracing paper.

Apply Design with Basting

1. If the design is not too large or complicated, it can be traced on to a piece of tissue paper; then this paper is pinned on to the material, at the exact place where you wish the embroidery to be. Unless you continue with your work right away, it may be

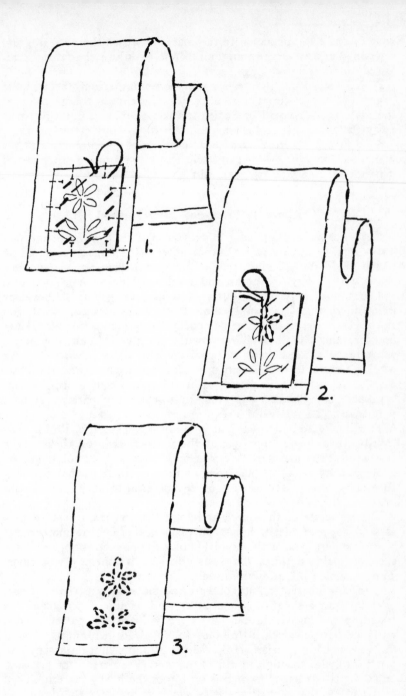

1.

2.

3.

wise to baste the paper on to the material where the pins are, and remove the pins as they might fall out or injure the fabric if allowed to remain too long.

2. Now sew over the design with a running stitch, through the paper and the material. Use a contrasting thread to the color of the material, so it will be easier for you to follow. Carefully tear away the tissue paper, before you start to do your crewel work.

3. You can do your crewel stitches over the running stitches which outline your design; this will cover the running stitches and it is not necessary to rip them out.

Apply by Prick-and-color Method

First get your supplies ready; you will need a long hat pin, heavy quality tracing paper, felt or other soft material for a pad on which to do the pricking, pounce powder, a pouncer, water color brush with a very fine point, and a tube of blue water color paint.

The pounce may be bought in a shop dealing with embroidery items or in an artists' supply shop. But if you cannot obtain it, you can make it by mixing some French chalk (non-perfumed talcum powder) and a little charcoal powder (to give it color, if you are working on a light color material on which the powdered chalk wouldn't show up). You can buy the French chalk and the powdered charcoal in a drugstore. Put this pounce in a shallow unbreakable dish, before you start to transfer the pattern, so you will have it all ready for use.

Then make a pouncer; this is a roll of flannel or felt. Roll it very tightly, then sew it together at the ends of the roll to keep the layers of material intact. Or you may have a blackboard eraser, made of felt; over this place one or two layers of flannel, then secure it by sewing at the ends of the material to keep the pouncer firm.

The principle of this prick-and-color method is to make a perforated copy of the design, then placing this on the material to be embroidered, through the little holes the pounce is applied, then the blue paint outlines the design formed by these perforations. This is shown in the illustrations:

1. Put a layer of felt or other thick material on a flat surface, over this put a sheet of tissue paper, and on top of this place the tracing paper on which you have already drawn the pattern. Now, with the hat pin prick little holes (about 1/16 inch apart) around the outline of the design. Hold the pin straight (not on a slant) to prick the holes through in a firm manner. The reason for pricking on to the tissue paper (which is on top of the heavy material, used as a pad) is that sometimes it is easier to transfer the design to

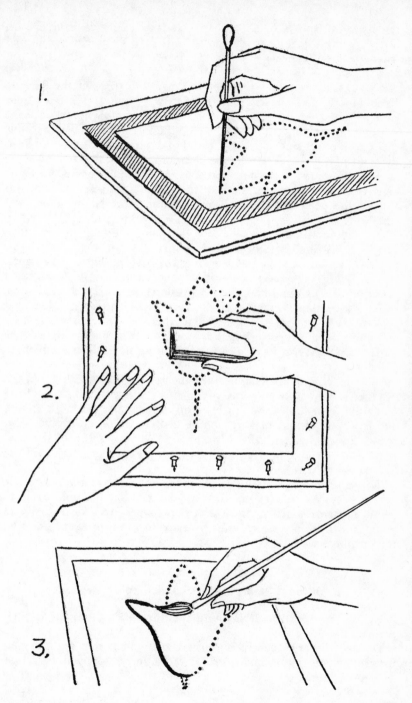

the material by use of tissue paper as it is easier to handle. But, if you want to transfer the design directly from the perforated tracing paper (especially a simple design and a small area) you may do so.

2. Lay out the material (on which you will transfer the design) on a smooth, flat surface. On top of this lay the perforated paper. Be sure you get the design in the exact position where you want it to be on the material. Then using thumb tacks or weights, put them around all sides of the material and perforated paper, to keep them firmly in place while the design is being transferred. One side of the paper may be rough, where the holes went through; usually this is the under side. If such is the case, lay the smooth side of the perforated paper down on the material, to avoid any smudging.

Dip the end of the pouncer into the pounce, shake it to remove surplus pounce as it is best not to apply it too thickly. In a light, circular motion, rub the pouncer over the perforations on the paper. Before doing the whole job, lift up one corner of the perforated paper and see if the dots are too light on the material. If that is so, rub a little more pounce over the perforated paper. If, when you have finished the task, you find that there is a surplus of pounce on the material, very lightly blow off the excess powder, as it is important that you have as clear a line as possible, on which to paint with the brush.

3. Use enough blue paint from the tube, mixed with water, to produce a light blue color. Experiment in mixing this, as too little paint might make it too watery and it will run on the material, and too much might make it too dark. Before you apply the paint to the material itself, do a little practicing on a scrap of material until you get the perfect mixture and the proper stroke of the brush you will use.

With the point of the brush, paint the outline over the dots made by the pounce. Be sure not to rest your arm on the dots so as to smudge them; place a piece of tissue paper over dots to avoid your arm touching them, while you are in the process of painting the outline.

Additional Pointers on Prick-and-color Method

Do not start embroidering until you are sure the paint is completely dry.

Do not discard the tracing paper on which you did the perforations; you may want to use the design on some other article at another time.

If you are transferring the design to a material of dark color, and the blue paint won't show on it, you may use white water color paint instead.

If you feel you are not sufficiently adept to handle a brush and water color paint, you might draw the outline of the design with a ball point pen. But, to make sure the ink does not run, first draw some lines on a scrap of the material, and wash the scrap under the faucet to test that the ink is color fast.

Apply with Carbon Paper

Ordinary typewriter carbon paper should not be used to transfer a design, as it is likely to smudge. Instead, buy dressmakers' carbon at a notion counter or dressmaker supply shop. Usually this carbon paper comes in blue and white; blue to be used on light color materials, and white to be used on dark materials.

Also have ready, for tracing the pattern, either a dry ball point pen or a metal knitting needle or a pencil with a very fine point. Masking tape is also suggested, or small weights, to hold down the work in the process of doing the transferring of design.

If you do not have a "straight eye" on which you can rely to get a design properly centered, it is wise for you to fold the material in half, and with your thumb and forefinger make a crease; then fold it in half in the other direction, and crease it down. Thus you have made four divisions and have a true center. If the material is too soft and won't show the crease, you could with a tape measure get the exact center of the material (in both directions) and run a basting stitch through as a guide. Be sure to use a thread of a color to contrast with the material, so you may easily see the basting.

Now make sure that you also have the true center of the design from which you are to transfer to the material, so you will get it in its proper position when it is traced through the carbon paper.

1. On a hard, flat surface (a table top or a board) lay the material, with its wrong side on the table or board. Keep the material smooth and flat, and use masking tape to hold it securely in place all around its four sides. If you do not use the tape, then place little weights around the four sides of the fabric, or perhaps use thumb tacks to keep it firm.

2. Match the center of the pattern to the center of the material, then spread the pattern over the maerial.

3. When you are sure you have the centers perfectly matched, with one hand hold down the design, and with your other hand very carefully slide in a piece of carbon paper between the ma-

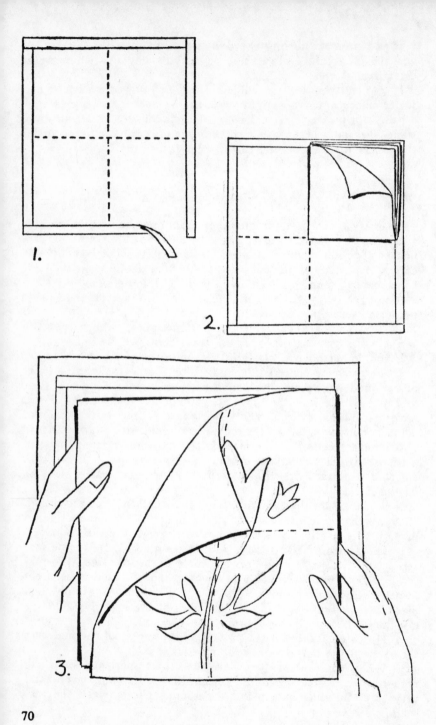

terial and the pattern; the carbon paper is to be face down on the material.

Carefully place little weights around the four sides of the design, being sure to keep your hands high so your wrist or fingers don't land on the design and make smudges through the carbon paper which is below it.

Some embroiderers also use masking tape around the design, rather than the weights. This is a matter of choice; but bear in mind it is a good idea occasionally to lift up a corner of the design and the carbon paper, to see how the work is progressing; it will be less convenient for you to do this if you use the tape rather than the weights.

When you are sure the material, the carbon and the pattern are properly in place, use your marking instrument (the pen, or knitting needle, or pencil) and bear down firmly on the design while you are tracing it. You might want to practice doing this on a scrap of material first, to find out how much pressure to exert, what instrument to use for tracing, so you may enjoy the best results in the transferring of the design and find out which method is most convenient for you.

Chapter Nine

THINGS YOU CAN MAKE

Now that crewel embroidery is a part of our contemporary scene, you can do a good deal of improvising about where and how to apply designs to things you wear and to items you use for accessorizing your home decorating.

Embroidery on Dress

A dress of simple line may be made to look expensive and individualistic with the addition of crewel work. A word of warning: do not attempt embroidery on a fabric that will not be long-lasting, as it would be wasteful to use thought and energy (and money) to do crewel work on something you would need to discard after one season's wearing. For that reason, too, it is wise not to do crewel work on a "high style" fashion, but to use it only on a simple, basic dress which remains in style throughout all the fickle changes of fashion.

As an example, here are shown two ways in which crewel work may be used on a dress of simple lines. Using a combination of basic embroidery stitches, a dress could have a border near the hem of the skirt. Or the embroidery could be sewed down the front of the dress. If more elaborate work is desired, you could use a scroll design with wavy lines, floral arrangements, and so on.

On a dress, it may be best to use just one color of yarn for embroidery, which is not too sharp a contrast to the dress material itself. Using more than one color of yarn may give the costume too "busy" a look. However, this is a matter of personal taste, and if you want to splurge with color on a garment, by all means express your individuality.

Accessory Jacket or Sweater

A bolero or other type of jacket, or a sweater, may be worn over more than one dress to produce an attractive costume. And this may be a good investment of crewel work. This could spark up an otherwise simple dress. Such a jacket or sweater could be made of simple fabric and subdued embroidery, and worn over day wear. Or it could be used for dress-up occasions when the jacket or sweater is made of a luxury fabric and the embroidery be of a more elaborate design.

Embroider a Bedspread

You may design an interesting spread for your bed. The simplest way is to embroider a border all around the edge of the bedspread, and you could use one of the simple basic decorative borders shown in Chapter Two, or devise a border of a floral or other continuous design.

If you want to make an all-over embroidery on the spread, here illustrated are two suggestions:

1. This is a geometrical design you could make in a combination of straight and double cross stitches.

2. Or you may like a design of this sort, which you could achieve with loop and straight stitches.

Either of the foregoing all-over stitches could be done in one color, or use yarns of two colors if you prefer.

1.

2.

3. This is a way of making squares, say 10 or 12 inches each square, which would make it easy for you to handle while embroidering. The illustration shows a seed stitch which is used around a leaf done with an outline stitch; or you could reverse the design and fill in the leaf with the seed stitches, and leave the area blank around the leaf. You could use one color (green preferably) for the leaf, and maybe another color for the seed stitches. When you have embroidered enough squares to make the bedspread, sew the squares together (seaming them on the wrong side by hand or machine stitch), and finishing on the right side (over the seams) with an outline stitch in a color to match the leaf.

In a bedspread made of squares, you might design two or three different kinds of squares (in floral or geometric patterns) and then alternate them when sewing them together.

3.

Table Cloths

Using the same ideas suggested for bedspreads, you could embroider a charming border around the table cloth, or perhaps make a center floral or bird design in it, or an all-over design. Table runners and place mats are also enhanced with embroidered borders.

A Bell Pull

You may not need a real pull to ring a bell, but it does make a pretty wall decoration, especially in some narrow space on a wall. These pulls are often used in interior decoration as a part of a grouping which includes pictures and mirrors. One usually associates a pull with traditional embroidery design; yet if you want to make one in contemporary design (to match your decorating theme) you may have fun in doing so.

The illustration shows a simple way of using a decorative border to go all the way down the length of the pull. At the pointed end, make a tassel, using the dominant color in the yarns you used for the embroidery. The way to make a tassel is shown in Chapter Two.

It is a good idea to use a sturdy lining on back of the pull so it hangs without puckering.

Drapery and Valance

You may produce rich-looking draperies and valances by using a decorative border, as suggested in this illustration. Or you may make your own design of all-over bird or floral or other design, either closely spaced or widely spaced, to suit your own decorating ideas.

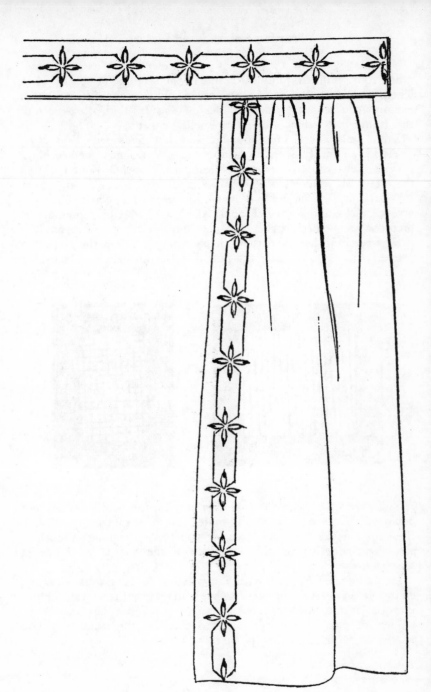

Framing Embroidered Picture

You may want to use some of your crewel work as pictures to grace your wall. First buy the frame of the size and style you want. Then, to mount the embroidery, cut a piece of smooth cardboard (or plywood) about ⅛ inch smaller on all sides than the groove of the frame into which the picture will be set.

Your embroidery must be flat and not puckered. You must stretch it smoothly over the cardboard. (Or you may need to block it first, for which instructions refer to Chapter Four.) When the picture is properly placed on the cardboard, use a strong pin or tiny tack at each of the four corners to keep it in place. Then put pins or tacks about ¼ inch apart all around the four sides of the picture, being sure to keep the embroidery smooth (and apply a little stretching here and there, if necessary). When the picture is properly in place, hammer the pins or tacks into the cardboard.

 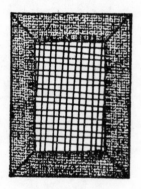

You may have some material overhanging the cardboard; do not cut it off, but turn it on to the under side of the board, and paste the edges of the material down, or you could use long stitches to sew them together on the underside of the board, as shown in illustrations.

It is a matter of choice with you whether to use a glass over the embroidered picture, or leave it without glass. Insert the picture into the frame, then proceed to put a protective backing on it, nailing or pasting the backing into place in the same way you would do with any other pictures you frame.